PASTORAL SUCCESSION PLAN

Oasis Church of South Florida Edition

GUY MELTON

Copyright © 2025 Guy Melton

ISBN: 978-0-9883311-6-7

Oasis Church of South Florida

All rights reserved.

CONTENTS

FOREWORD _____ I

PREFACE _____ V

INTRODUCTION: THE OASIS STORY _____ IX

CHAPTER 1 - THE US CHURCH TRANSITION OF PASTORS _____ 1

CHAPTER 2 - THE BIBLICAL TRANSITION OF SPIRITUAL LEADERS _ 17

CHAPTER 3 - IS PASTORAL RETIREMENT BIBLICAL? _____ 25

CHAPTER 4 - THE PASSING OF THE BATON _____ 31

CHAPTER 5 - TIMELINES ARE CRUCIAL _____ 35

CHAPTER 6 - COMMUNICATION _____ 45

CHAPTER 7 - THE ROLE OF THE CHURCH COUNCIL _____ 49

CHAPTER 8 - FUTURE MINISTRY ASSIGNMENTS _____ 53

CHAPTER 9 - SENIOR PASTOR'S COMMITMENT TO THE CHURCH, LEADERSHIP, AND LEAD PASTOR _____ 57

CHAPTER 10 - NEXT STEPS _____ 61

CONCLUSION: ROOTS _____ 65

APPENDIX _____ 71

BIBLIOGRAPHY _____ 81

FOREWORD

Oasis Church: A Church Loving All Nations Over Time.

Every time I enter the Sanctuary of Oasis Church, I have a profound sense of connection to my brothers and sisters in the church and around the world. As I watch the people enter the Oasis building, I can hardly hold back my tears of joy. The flags above always make me proud to have been a small part of such a remarkable gathering of authentic believers in Jesus. To me, Oasis is a living example of loving all people and all nations.

Over 30 years ago, when Guy and Tonia told me they were "going West" to plant a church, I was sad to be "losing" from our team such a gifted and blessed couple. When they told me they would be going toward Flamingo Road, I was happy they would be close by!

When their dream of going west became a reality, Flamingo Road was considered by folks in Hollywood and Miramar as "The End of the World." Who would have guessed the world would come to Flamingo Road and into Oasis Church?

Over the years, I have seen over a hundred attempts to plant new churches. What I saw happening at Oasis was unique. Oasis opened its doors to the world, and the world showed up. Oasis showed us all a new way to be the church for all people.

I have known Guy and Tonia for almost my entire life. They are perfectly gifted at loving all people equally, and I have never known them to fail to love everyone.

The mark of a great church is the quality of its love over time. Oasis Church has clearly received and released Jesus' love over time. The DNA of Jesus' love must continue to grow and thrive as the church transitions into its coming future. The coming leaders have been mentored and prepared at Oasis for this new delivery of Jesus' love.

I have been inspired over the years by this quote from author E. Stanley Jones who was a Methodist missionary to India for 55 years.

He said, "Love is calling me. I need to go."

As we move through our lives, we will hear love calling us to go. The succession process at Oasis will test all involved. As long as Jesus is heard and obeyed, Oasis Church will continue to love and keep perfecting that love over time.

As Oasis finishes its succession plans for the future, Pam and I will look on with joy because *love never fails*.

I know the people of the world that Oasis has received, will be up to receiving the new world that is still coming to Flamingo Road and Oasis Church.

Even from heaven, we will watch Oasis Church loving all people.

Love is calling Oasis Church. Oasis needs to go forward loving over time.

-Bud and Pam McCord

Mountain View Hotel

PREFACE

I embarked on this book on pastoral succession—my own—from where much of our ministry began: Gatlinburg, Tennessee. It was here that Tonia and I honeymooned in 1975 while we were still college students in Atlanta.

As bright-eyed newlyweds, we stayed in the Mountain View Hotel, an old historic hotel at the entrance of Gatlinburg, which I will mention later in the book.

While it was torn down in 1993 to make way for progress for an amusement park, the park did not make it, and today it's nothing but a parking lot. This morning, I am sitting in that same parking lot, watching the excited tourists dashing toward the main parkway in Gatlinburg. I've done it many times myself and then with our boys as they grew up.

However, this morning, I began a journey that will ultimately bring me full circle in my pastoral ministry of almost 50 years. As 19-year-old kids staying in this old, worn, dated, but still popular hotel, we were unaware of what God had in store for us.

I couldn't think of a better place to start writing than this parking lot, where our journey began five decades ago.

As we approach our 50th Year of Marriage on June 26th, 2025, which is still hard to get my head around, I can't help but reflect on what a ride it's been! If I had to do it again, I would still do it with my high school sweetheart in a heartbeat—the one who is still 'my babe,' Tonia.

Since this is an in-house project, it seems more appropriate to open this preface using the words of another pastor who has successfully worked through a pastoral succession plan.

His book was the first I had ever read or heard on pastoral succession, although I now realize there are a few others. His story felt so much like mine, having planted the church he was transitioning from, so please let me use his words to begin our journey through this *Church Edition* of what I am encouraging us to consider.

> *While on sabbatical in the summer of 2012, I read Bob Russell's great book, Transition Plan. The premise of the*

book revolves around the process of a pastor approaching the elders about a succession plan. He wrote that when the elders approach the pastor about a succession plan, it is a firing plan. But, when the pastor approaches the elders about a succession plan, it is truly a succession plan. I had been the pastor of Johnson Ferry Baptist Church (JFBC) for 30 years in 2012. The milestone of taking on my fourth decade in ministry got my attention. As one of the Big 10 goals that God had put on my heart for the fourth decade at JFBC, I set the goal of developing a succession plan with the church elders. We began this discussion in 2013.

Initially, they were surprised. I was only 60 years old. The church was doing well. I was the only pastor the church had ever had, and every staff member had come to Johnson Ferry under my leadership. Just bringing up the topic caught them by surprise. In many ways, it was a surprise to me as well. A part of me still saw myself as the young pastor planting a new church in the North Atlanta suburbs. Obviously, those days were over.

Bryant Wright

Succession: Preparing Your Ministry for the Next Lead[1]

---

[1] Bryant Wright, *Succession: Preparing Your Ministry for the Next Leader* (Erscheinungsort nicht ermittelbar: B&H Books, 2022); Vonna Laue, "Creating a Successful Succession Plan," Church Law & Tax, July 26, 2016, https://www.churchlawandtax.com/stay-legal/governance/creating-a-successful-succession-plan/.

INTRODUCTION

The Oasis Story

The story of Bryant Wright is very close to my own and that of Oasis. Nothing in my life gives me greater joy outside my own family and marriage than to have served this *baby* church these past 33 years.

Now, as I write the preamble and rough copy of my own and the Oasis succession journey, I can't think of a better place to share my heart with you than here in the mountains of Tennessee in and around Gatlinburg where Tonia and I first visited as 19-year-old newlyweds. I write now from Chalet Village, where we first had a tiny, 1000 square foot, 2-bedroom-and-bath home that we'd called a cabin. That cabin later burned down. God allowed us to build a much nicer, more modern one with a fitting reminder of its journey in the saying "beauty for ashes" on one of its walls today. Here, my mind wanders to the parking lot of the old hotel we visited on our honeymoon at the end of the main street in Gatlinburg; the hotel that is now history and nothing but an old, deserted amusement park that closed many years ago and remains vacant. I also think of the trail along the river into the National Park and the Blue Ridge Parkway, where I've had so many prayer walks and some of the most somber moments over the years of just me, the meandering brook, nature, and God.

There are so many significant events. Ministries would shape my ministry and Oasis Church from these locations. Phone calls were received here of staff infidelity, calls of unhappy leaders leaving while I was on vacation (and even once during a cruise), and calls of moral failure by volunteers. There were also weeks of fasting, reading books, sabbaticals, and meetings to reconcile with those who had left poorly or because of private immorality.

God's leading to significant decisions that have impacted thousands at Oasis (and others) over the years through the **Bike for Haiti** (BFH) and **Love Cities, Love Pastors** (LCLP) initiatives—and many of the ministries that we've undertaken— were birthed here in the mountains of East

Tennessee and the Great Smokey Mountains National Park.

Over the years, I've led you to 7-NOW, three campuses, up to 14 services a week, a multi-cultural ministry that might be among the most diverse in the USA. I've also led you to LCLP, the Oasis Beach House, our current building, team teaching, and many others. God matured and confirmed many of these endeavors in and around Gatlinburg and the Great Smokies.

Most of them took months and sometimes years for God to cement in my heart. Our yearly visits to the mountains inspired the birth of Christmas at the Oasis. The lights and displays, the multitudes here, sparked the desire to replicate them at CATO over the years. While some worked and some didn't, they all germinated in these parts of Tennessee.

How appropriate that I am writing in these very spots, yet another chapter, another season, another huge step of faith not only in my ministry but also for the future generations of those who will lead Oasis Church well beyond my years.

Thousands of pages have been written here, many of them born into books and delivered. Why now write this final chapter? It is not for the masses, not even for others outside our church to read (although it might help serve some churches in the future in writing their story).

I hate writing (it's painful, vulnerable, scary, and risky) since it's one thing to say something but another to write it on paper where it is memorialized forever, for better or worse. No, I have never enjoyed writing; I also know that I say so much and speak so much that it begins to feel "blah, blah blah," and the details and my heart might get missed in my feeble attempt to share something that I think is of utmost importance and something that God has given me to share. I've never seen myself as a great verbal or written communicator, but I've tried to do my best to use what I have and make the best of it coming from my heart.

This succession plan for Oasis and me is yet another attempt. As with any devotional, article, email, or book I've written, I always fear, tremble, and even feel uneasiness about whether anyone will read it. Yet . . . I write.

I've often explained to staff and others that whether someone reads a devotion or pastoral email is not essential to me, but at least they have the information. If they choose not to read it, I've done my part, and it's there if they ever want to know why I or Oasis did this or that. Trust me, there are a million topics I could have written a book about over the years for my ego or even to try to establish funding for myself. However, the books I have written are only because I could not, not write them. They were impressed and impregnated into my heart and soul. I hoped that God would not allow me to write them. While

I'm always honored and humbled that anyone would take the time and part of their life to hear or read a word from me, the most important thing is that I'd be obedient to God. To tell you that I am *appreciative* is to use too small a word for anyone who reads this. I'm so grateful. Hopefully, the future generations of Oasis will be thankful you did, and most importantly, that we followed God's leading in this transitional process for Oasis Church.

I feel like Paul did as he wrote what he knew would be his last letter to the churches. He wanted to ensure they heard some things and that he was ready for a transition. Trust me, I'm not Paul. I know that. But as I write these pages, that last letter is at the forefront of my mind and heart.

> "... and the time for my departure is near. I have fought the good fight, I have finished the race, I have kept the faith."
>
> **2 Timothy 4-6-7**

> "What you heard from me, keep as the pattern of sound teaching, with faith and love in Christ Jesus. Guard the good deposit that was entrusted to you—guard it with the help of the Holy Spirit who lives in us."
>
> 2 Timothy 1:13-14

Cathartic

I am sharing my story of ministry and Oasis for several reasons. And maybe it's more for me. Perhaps it's to set the table of why I feel this decision and journey is important; maybe it's to help prepare those who do not understand, will not, or have not been on our Oasis journey for a long time. For any of these reasons (or even some I haven't even thought of), I will spend some time introducing this next season in my life and the life of Oasis.

There is no retirement in the Bible, and I will NOT retire. I'll *reposition* for this season for the benefit of Oasis and the Kingdom.

I could stay . . . I think till I die. I can fake my energy; I can coast. (I've never been willing to coast.) Humanly, I can feel more significant by staying. I can always wake up knowing where I will serve and work and at what time, with vacations and a solid paycheck. But that is not my calling. And *that* has never been either what pastoral calling was about in the New Testament.

CHAPTER 1

The US Church Transition of Pastors

"A few years ago, I knew three ministries that all experienced a tragedy unexpectedly striking their senior leaders. Two of those leaders passed away suddenly, and one was diagnosed with an aggressive form of cancer. Each organization scrambled to find solutions; some were better prepared than others. It was an eye-opening experience for

me, as an outsider, to consider what should be learned from their difficulties." [2]

A prominent church with more than 25,000 members rapidly eroded into a congregation of less than 250 with dwindling finances—and its rapid demise traces back to a problem many churches unfortunately face today: the lack of a pastoral succession plan.[3]

Yes, these are just a few horror stories of pastoral transitions.

The Church in America has some serious issues with pastoral turnover. Recently, I read a book titled *Tsunami* by Samuel R. Chand and Scott Wilson[4], which predicts that at least 30 percent (and I think it could be more) of pastors from the boomer generation will retire or leave the ministry in just a few short years. We have seen it coming for many years.

I have often told myself and other pastors, "Wow, it's going to get rough, especially in the mega-churches (those with a thousand attenders or more), as most of the pastors in many of these US mega-churches are in the baby boom generation. The experience, gifting, and qualities required

---

[2] Laue, "Creating a Successful Succession Plan."

[3] Erika E. Cole, "Pastoral Succession Plans: Why Your Church Needs One," Church Law & Tax, March 9, 2017, https://www.churchlawandtax.com/stay-legal/governance/succession-plans-why-your-church-needs-one/.

[4] Samuel R Chand and Scott Wilson, *Tsunami: Open Secrets to Pastoral Succession & Transition*, n.d.

to lead a church of 50-90 regular attenders differ considerably from those needed to lead a large church. Yes, the church is a ministry. Oasis is no different in our Vision and Mission today (with 2,000 members and over 4,000 more that call us their home) than in September of 1991 when we gathered with our core group of 9 adults, Tonia and me. The same mission still drives us today. Our DNA has not changed. Many churches often see their mission, core values, and DNA change with time, much because of the rapid turnover of pastors. It is the national average for a pastor to stay for 4-5 years. That means many pastors leave 2 and 3 years into the ministry.

Barna Group, the most respected research and polling group in the American Church of over 400,000 Christian Churches, published in 2017[5] some concerning statistics on the topic still being quoted today:

- Pastors 40 and under dropped by 50% in the last ten years.
- The number of pastors, age 55, doubled.
- Pastors aged 65 and older have nearly tripled.

Finding a new pastor takes about two years for a megachurch with over one thousand attendees. During that

---

[5] "The Aging of America's Pastors," Barna Group, accessed January 14, 2025, https://www.barna.com/research/aging-americas-pastors/.

time, attendance, offerings, and the ministry usually decline.

In the same book mentioned above, Samuel R. Chand and Scott Wilson indicate that 90 percent of all churches have no succession plan for when their pastor leaves, retires, dies, or has some medical condition that incapacitates him.

They mention an undisputed statistic: **_100 percent_ of all pastors will stop pastoring**.

Since our beginning, the Oasis's Senior and Lead Pastor roles have never changed. Many in our church know no other pastor but me. But many who have no Christian church background have no clue how or what it means to say goodbye to one pastor and welcome another.

This will be an entirely new experience for many. Two generations of Oasisers were born, have grown up, married, and served here. Many more in this younger generation, currently in nursery, preschool, elementary, and teens, will be impacted by the succession from one pastor to another. How we handle this transition means so much to these future generations of Oasis Church.

In my opinion, *how* we do it matters little to most of the church. If you show them a church constitution and tell them this is how it's done and has been done for several hundred years by thousands of churches, then that is good enough for them.

However, the reason the transferring of the baton in so many churches fails and pastors come and go like a revolving wheel on a merry-go-round is how we, as a culture, transition from one pastor to another. I do not believe it is biblical.

Let me give a small illustration of how it works in all the churches I have known (including the one I grew up in, served 13 years on staff, and was sent by to plant Oasis Church in 1991):

When a Pastor announces his departure, the church board or the pastor himself announces it to the church. Immediately, the legal board, whether it'd be deacons, trustees, elders—or, in our case, the Church Council—forms a Pulpit Committee. Sometimes, a combination of all kinds of members is nominated, chosen, voted on, and thrown into a committee to make the most significant decision the church will ever make.

This "Pulpit Committee" may comprise of the most popular, longest attending, legacy family member, or best-looking. In most cases, this team may not even know each other. Some may not be in leadership or even in concert with the values and mission of the Church. This does not mean this is true about all; most are good, well-meaning people.

The pastor packs his bags and rides off into the sunset of either retirement, another church, or any number of assignments he may go to.

From there, the committee begins to solicit prospects' names. (With our online presence, we have been known to receive over 200 applications and resumes when we have just a regular job opening at Oasis—which is crazy to me.)

Then, the group splits the list of potential candidates and starts sending emails or calling these unknown persons.

After months—or, in most cases, a year to two years—they whittle down the list. They narrow it down to maybe 5 or 10 candidates. Then, they visit churches they might pastor, which are as far away as a plane can take them. They begin to interview and do background checks. They ask people who have been given by the applicant as references as if they would share the truth with the new church. Most of the time, they are presently pastoring, so all this must be kept secret, which hamstrings the team from really doing their job of finding an excellent objective background. So how do you find out and know you are getting the person you think they are? Well, you don't in this scenario.

Finally, you have chosen three to four candidates, and the committee begins to interview them in any number of ways: asking church members, maybe having them speak, or sending a group undercover to their present church to hear them speak, which is always awkward.

Finally, a tired and weary team that started with great excitement and has seen many bumps along the way says, "Let's just decide. We need a pastor, and we are long overdue."

The gravity of this decision is palpable. There are 1001 details to hammer out—decisions, negotiations, obstacles, and pitfalls you can't plan on in the final sprint to the new pastor. And the excitement of finding the right candidate is not enough.

Once the committee knows who their man is, they take them to the church. They parade them and their family around. Have meet-and-greets as if people can understand who they are getting.

More than anything, a popularity show of looks, speaking from the pulpit, and personality wins the day. Don't get me wrong; the people are all well-meaning, for the most part. They want God's will. They are praying for God's will.

But at best, humanly speaking, it's a risk or a considerable gamble if this person works out.

I have told our staff many times that we should start from within Oasis when we search to fill a position. Let's start with people who love our church and mission and have already invested their lives in it. We know them, and we love them too. However, we also often know their weaknesses, and they might bias us against hiring them instead of that shiny object online with all the best resume writing skills.

As I remind our team, hiring anyone from inside or outside is risky. At Oasis, the best team members and longest-serving staff have all come from within our church. If this approach has proven effective for our team, why not consider it for the Lead Pastor role?

It may not always be possible for various reasons, but I still think it is the best and biblical way.

Remember when the church was young and growing by the hundreds and thousands, and the disciples were over their heads? What did they do? Did they put out a cry in the Jerusalem Post or the Antioch Times about their need for pastors, deacons, and leaders? Did they post the job openings on the walls of the court and temple? Did they go to the leading theological schools or contact the most well-known rabbi? No, they didn't. One reason is there was no history of hiring platforms or venues. LOL. But what did they do? They said, "Let us search among us. Let us find these qualified people." No, not those candidates with schooling or tenure, but qualified *biblically*.

Our American way is more like hiring a CEO. For churches of our size, yes, the pastor needs to be part businessman or CEO in some respects; however, the overwhelming call is for a pastor qualified by the New Testament.

The American church dates someone for a few weeks or months. They know little about them and then marry, only to divorce a few years later. We would not recommend a dating relationship and marriage to a young couple that just met, yet the church does this repeatedly to get the same results.

Recently, I met with a pastor in California who had pastored a church for 25 years and recently transitioned out as Lead Pastor. He turned the church over to a man who grew up there and had served as a youth pastor for years.

This pastor friend recounted that when he first arrived at this church, the head deacon came to him and told him how, before this pastor's arrival, he'd had to go five times in 10 years to the local denomination association to ask them to remove or replace their pastor. This deacon pleaded with him not to leave. He said he would never serve again because he could not go through another pastoral transition as a deacon. Two weeks before the pastor turned over the Lead Pastor role to the younger man in the church, that deacon died. On his deathbed, the pastor said his deacon told him, "I'm thankful I never had to have another pastor in my lifetime." The next day, he died, and two weeks later, my friend made his transition out of his Lead Pastor role. What a sad story that any layperson should go through repeated pastoral turnover with all the accompanying pains. Yet, I also can't help but see the beautiful last chapter in this deacon's story, having had one pastor for the rest of his life—his last twenty-five years.

I can't even tell you how many train wrecks I have watched happen and continue to happen when you hire a new pastor in the way I just described. It would probably take a book of a thousand pages to give you all the harmful results of doing it the American way, not the New Testament and Biblical way.

Let me share just one last story that is close to home. I'll try not to be too personal, although it happened at my home church, which sent us to plant Oasis.

Our church was approaching 50 years old. It had seen three pastors come and go: the founder I sat under as a kid, the founder's son-in-law who had an enormous ministry in Miami and was highly thought of, and the third . . . a young pastor who had accepted Christ, been baptized, married, and sent out as a missionary from within the same church. When the second pastor decided to leave, the church did the typical search, except they included a few senior staff members with long tenures. This created a lot of issues, and none were good. However, this is not the story. The church settled on one of their kids. They loved him, and he loved them. They brought him back from the mission field, and he served as Lead Pastor for 18 years before God called him back to missions.

It was after these 18 years that the next search began. They opted for the traditional search mode. They found the man. He was qualified, had a PhD, a beautiful family, and a fancy sports car, and they were the perfect look for a large, prestigious church. They came with good recommendations. They courted them, and they came. I know it well since I was part of the crisis management once he left.

Three weeks into the new pastorate, he turned on the departing pastor. The new guy convinced this church—where the leaving pastor grew up and pastored for 18 years and served as their missionary for eight years before then—that they could not financially or spiritually support him. The incoming guy contrived lies and things that I did not believe could be possible and have been well-proven since. The pain the church and the long-tenured pastor and his wife went through is something that scarred them, me, and the church I loved and where this missionary pastor spent most of his life serving.

Within two years, the new pastor had not only shut the leaving pastor, ruined his good name, and turned lifelong friends against him but also changed the name of the church and its constitution and ran off around 80-90 percent of their beloved staff, many of whom had grown up in the church.

I have seen few things worse than that in my almost 50 years of ministry. Not only did he crush the former Lead pastor, but he almost crushed the church. The church had about one thousand attenders when the shiny pastor finally left, or I should say when he finally tore it apart, ripping the heart out of the once large, growing congregation. This congregation, written about in books as one of the largest and fastest-growing churches in the nation, was now down to about 200 in an auditorium that would seat over 2000 people.

Oasis Church, the baby of this injured church during that time, became a lifeline to help them not die. I spoke there. Oasis sent offerings to them, we lent them our worship teams, and we met with their destitute and hurting leadership. This is but the tip of the iceberg of what went on.

I will leave you with this one last piece of the story. The same pastor who was responsible for such hurt went from there to one of the largest oldest churches in north central Florida and did the same thing. He was run out of town after he split the church. He took 750 people with him and started another church. It almost killed the original congregation. They had called me before accepting him as a pastor, hearing I had opinions about him and what he did at my home church. I was honest. But they did not listen; the shiny objects, beautiful faces, and articulate tongues took them down, too. Sad but true.

There are thousands of stories of pastoral transitions that did not work out. Seldom, though, does this happen when the leadership looks within, and the Lead Pastor is involved in the process if they are a long-tenured or founding pastor. Why? Because there is a more *biblical* way.

In the next chapter, we will discuss the biblical passing of the baton from one pastor to another. To set the stage, I'd like us to examine two types of constitutions of the traditional way of succession, with our Oasis' constitution being one of them.

The Oasis Constitution and Bylaws

Duties of Officers

Article V Section 1

A) The Senior Pastor or his appointed representative shall preach the Gospel regularly and shall be at liberty to preach the whole counsel of the Word of God as the Lord leads him. The Senior Pastor shall determine the time for the administration of the ordinances of the Church, act as moderator at all Church meetings for the transaction of Church matters, supervise the teaching ministries of the Church, and tenderly watch over the spiritual interests of the membership.

(B) The Senior Pastor shall appoint the members of the various non-elected committees. He shall be an ex-officio member of all committees, boards, and organizations of the Church. He shall serve as the president of the corporation. He shall publicly inform all newly-elected officers of the particular function and the responsibilities of their respective offices. He shall extend the right hand of fellowship to all new members on behalf of the Church and perform such other duties as generally appertain to such a position. The Senior Pastor shall be free to choose the means and methods by which he exercises the ministry that God has given him.

From the Presbyterian Church of America (PCA)

20-2. Every church should be under the pastoral oversight of a minister, and when a church has no pastor it should seek to secure one without delay.

A church shall proceed to elect a pastor in the following manner: The Session shall call a congregational meeting to elect a pulpit committee which may be composed of members from the congregation at large or the Session, as designated by the congregation (see *BCO* 25). The pulpit committee shall, after consultation and deliberation, recommend to the congregation a pastoral candidate who, in its judgment, fulfills the Constitutional requirements of that office (e.g., *BCO* 8, 13-6 and 21) and is most suited to be profitable to the spiritual interests of the congregation (cf. *BCO* 20-6).

CHAPTER 2

The Biblical Transition of Spiritual Leaders

The corporate handoff of leadership from one pastor to another in American churches is not working and is becoming more of an issue than ever before.

Why have we not spent more time studying and following the biblical transition and baton handoff? I am not qualified to answer this, but after 46 years in full-time ministry, I have some ideas.

As I've shown in the previous chapter, the church often operates more like a democracy or a business than it does a family or the Family of God with parental leadership. Someone can debate this but look back at the Presbyterian Church of America Constitution and our Oasis Constitution.

Our church considered approximately 20 different types of churches before our editor, Bob Goodwin, drew up a phenomenal Church Constitution that has served us well for 33 years. However, the only thing we knew as a core group was how other American churches did it, as well as the Baptist churches that most of the founding group grew up in.

We tweaked ours and got the best of all of them. However, you must stretch and contort to see the biblical basis of pastoral successions and transfer to a new pastor. It's not bad at all. It has a lot of good qualities, but it's still more our culture and business style of leadership, which has little biblical example or premise.

We can argue this, and I can support both sides. However, given the state of our world and the size of Oasis, I think that, at this time in the world we live in, we should look more at the Biblical model than the American model in our ministry.

In his book *Where Will the Mantle Fall? A Biblical and Legal Guide to Succession Planning*[6], attorney and pastor Travell Travis uses many great analogies of the Bible's great transitions.

- **Moses handed the baton to his protégé, Joshua. (Numbers 27:18-21)**
- **David handed the Building of the Temple to Solomon. (1 Chronicles 28:11)**
- **Elijah passed the mantle to Elisha. (2 Kings 2:13-15)**
- **Jesus handed the Keys of His Kingdom to His Disciples. (Matthew 16:18-20)**

These are some beautiful examples of passing the baton biblically from one spiritual leader to another.

They were all great successes.

The baton passing has been going on for thousands of years, and the Bible has many good examples. God is a God of planning, process, and order. Why should the church be different?

---

[6] Torrino Travell Travis, *Where Will the Mantle Fall? A Biblical and Legal Guide to Succession Planning*, n.d.

Anytime I begin something new or feel burdened to do something, I first pray about it. Then, I search my heart and the Scriptures to make sure it's biblical.

Sometimes, biblical words are not written on the proverbial wall; however, the Holy Spirit will always show me a place in the Bible that explains the principle to confirm it or may do just the opposite and convince me that it is *not* what God wants.

It might be the greatest idea, yet it might not be biblical or God's will.

I find that a succession plan in a local church is not only important but also biblical. I am convinced the most biblical plan is to have one generation hand off to the next within the congregation.

Every succession and handoff in the Bible were not always God's will or success, but God blessed the ones where we know God's hand was in.

Interestingly, on my first day, as I began this time of study and writing, my devotional Scripture was **2 Kings 1-2, 2:9-16.** Yes, the story of the succession of Elijah to Elisha. This was no coincidence.

> *When they had crossed, Elijah said to Elisha, "Tell me, what can I do for you before I am taken from you?"*

"Let me inherit a double portion of your spirit," Elisha replied.

"You have asked a difficult thing," Elijah said, *"yet if you see me when I am taken from you, it will be yours—otherwise, it will not."*

As they were walking along and talking together, suddenly a chariot of fire and horses of fire appeared and separated the two of them, and Elijah went up to heaven in a whirlwind. Elisha saw this and cried out, "My father! My father! The chariots and horsemen of Israel!" And Elisha saw him no more. Then he took hold of his garment and tore it in two.

Elisha then picked up Elijah's cloak that had fallen from him and went back and stood on the bank of the Jordan. He took the cloak that had fallen from Elijah and struck the water with it. "Where now is the Lord, the God of Elijah?" he asked. When he struck the water, it divided to the right and to the left, and he crossed over.

The company of the prophets from Jericho, who were watching, said, "The spirit of Elijah is resting on Elisha." And they went to meet him and bowed to the ground before him.

> ***"Look," they said, "we your servants have fifty able men . . . " (2 Kings 2:9-16)***

One of the interesting things about this is that the Bible records 50 men who supported and believed in Elisha as he took the mantle of Elijah. It's wonderful when God places the church's next leaders within the congregation, and the church already believes in them, loves them, and supports them. They are family.

The same day, my New Testament reading and devotional were **Luke 24**, Jesus on the road to Emmaus as He worked His succession plan out. Not everyone could see it. It took some time. It took faith. Even the followers of Christ struggled with His leaving and the 12 taking the mantle. It was not a smooth transition, for sure. It was messy, just as we humans are.

Transitions are about following God's calling and will, whether it benefits or makes us happy. Jesus was not about making His disciples and followers comfortable or happy. Happiness comes from following Him, knowing Him, and being in the center of His will.

Talking about filling some big shoes (or at that time, sandals.) How do you think the disciples would have felt if they had been told they had to fill the sandals of Jesus? They probably would've said: "Nope, that ain't happening."

No, Jesus in **Mathew 28** gave them their own shoes and said to them now walk in them and fill your shoes, your mission, and your calling.

Paul chose Timothy as his mentee for ministry, which was beautiful. Barnabas chose to mentor Paul, and then the church chose from within Paul and Barnabas to be sent out. This is biblical succession and transition the way it should be.

> *After proclaiming the Message in Derbe and establishing a strong core of disciples, they retraced their steps to Lystra, then Iconium, and then Antioch, putting grit in the lives of the disciples, urging them to stick with what they had begun to believe and not quit, making it clear to them that it wouldn't be easy: "Anyone signing up for the kingdom of God has to go through plenty of hard times.*
>
> *Paul and Barnabas handpicked leaders in each church. After praying—their prayers intensified by fasting—they presented these new leaders to the Master to whom they had entrusted their lives . . . (Acts 14:21-26 MSG)*

Transitions and successions are NOT about filling shoes. They are about *fulfilling God's call* upon one's life.

There is NOTHING in Scripture that says one leader following another fills their shoes—whether they be Joshua, Elisha, Solomon, the Disciples, or you and me. It is about doing God's will for the person involved and the Church of Christ Jesus.

CHAPTER 3

Is Pastoral Retirement Biblical?

This should be the smallest chapter. But if you know me, you'd know I may have a few more things to add.

Simply said, **there is no retirement for men called to ministry**. I have no Scripture or stories to give you to support the argument for pastors to go into retirement.

There are new chapters of life and ministry, maybe. There are seasons, yes.

There are *re-assignments*.

There are *re-alignments*.

Re-positioning.

Re-treading.

New roles.

I met recently with the founding pastor of one of the largest churches in Southwest Florida, Dennis Gingerich, of Cape Christian Church in Cape Coral. I was surprised at how similar our paths have been and how close his church's history is to ours at Oasis. I found a great sense of unity in spirit with him. In our almost full day of conversation, he reconfirmed the direction we are headed as Oasis is the right way to go. He could not imagine doing succession the way traditional American churches do it. He has been on this pastoral transition journey for 13 years and has said several times that he has NO regrets. That was very affirming and encouraging.

Dennis is a pastor who left his Senior Pastor role very early. He still serves on the team at Cape Christian and just recently left his full-time new role he's been serving in to go part-time. He speaks to retirement and the wrestling with the assumption most have when a senior or founding pastor steps out of his role for several reasons. I'll give you what he says directly from his blog entry, Two Words That Make Me Angry[7]:

- **I Devalue Retirement.** I have come to realize my thoughts are counter-cultural. Most every working American looks forward to the day they can sit and do nothing. Not me. Fishing, boating or golfing doesn't appeal to me. Even my hobby of photography doesn't look good as a full-time option. I guess I've watched too many retirees move to Florida and get super depressed. In fact, as a police chaplain, I know the inside story. Every year, dozens of retirees in our city commit suicide. No purpose. No meaning. No hope. Nothing to get out of bed for in the morning. In contrast, I love what I do. I love seeing the transformation of lives. I love helping the team take new territory. When someone thinks I've retired, that isn't a positive step for me. I've watched as people obsess about their retirement date—count it down on their smartphones; talk about it every single day to every person they meet; and they let up on the accelerator, put it in neutral and slowly coast to a stop. Now, I plan to slow down and decrease the

---

[7] DGINGERICH, "Two Words That Made Me Angry," *Successful Successions* (blog), December 10, 2019, https://successfulsuccessions.com/two-words-that-made-me-angry/.

amount of time I spend in the office a few years from now. But for someone to think that I retired at age 55 when I implemented the succession plan by moving out of the driver's seat and taking another seat on the bus, goes completely against my values—because I don't value retirement as my ultimate goal.

- **I Discovered That Few Understand the Cost.** As I reflected with my counselor, I realized that a significant part of my internal anger at the *"How's retirement?"* question had to do with something I hadn't verbalized publicly. I was angry that people potentially thought that I was so well-positioned with my financial resources that I could just choose not to work anymore and be set for the rest of my life. That bothered me more than I was aware. Quite the opposite. By giving up the highest-paid position in the organization, I've significantly sacrificed financial security. And there have been plenty of other less measurable costs to my ego by giving up control and taking a much less visible role in the organization I founded. But I'm still convinced it was the right decision. I have absolutely no regrets. And the organization has prospered greatly because of the implementation of a succession plan.

Of course, since one hundred percent of pastors leave or die, there is a transition. We all die, we all get old, and we all slow down.

I read one pastor who said, **"We are all interim pastors."** We are only filling the role for a season, with some seasons being longer than others.

I will discuss transitions in the following chapters. But let me finish this one by highlighting that I do not believe retirement is biblical. It is another concept of American or European culture that man invented. It is not bad, but one thing I know: it's not Biblical because pastoring is not a career. It's a calling.

I WILL NOT be retiring.

CHAPTER 4

The Passing of the Baton

"You did not choose me, but I chose you and appointed you so that you might go and bear fruit—fruit that will last—and so that whatever you ask in my name the Father will give you." (John 15:16)

That His fruit will remain should be one of the most compelling reasons to have a well-thought-out and Biblical succession plan from one spiritual shepherd to the next.

As most know, if you have followed track and field, whether in high school or the Olympics, there is no more crucial time during a relay than the baton handoff. The seconds leading up to and after the pass often determine who wins or loses a relay. It's not just about who's the fastest, swiftest, or has the best mechanics and talent. It's mainly about the baton.

If you equate that to the church, this is probably the weakest moment and part of a transition. For most churches, there isn't even a handoff. One runner (or pastor) leaves the baton on the track in hopes the next one who follows will find it. If they do, they pick it up and keep the same pace, not missing a beat. If this sounds ridiculous . . . it is!

My desire is that Oasis gets the baton handoff right, not for me or the next Lead Pastor but for the body of Christ at Oasis, the Kingdom, and the many souls in our South Florida area who look to our church for light and spiritual guidance.

I ran a little track in High School. Truth be told, I did not want to. I wouldn't say I liked it and wasn't very good at it. However, my football and basketball coaches often coached track, too, so they would pressure me to run. I can tell you there was nothing the coaches worked harder on than that baton handoff.

Why should the church be any different?

In the Bible examples we have mentioned, along with many others over thousands of years, we see some fantastic baton handoffs to the next leader, king, priest, politician, and spiritual leaders and pastors.

While we will not dwell on the ones who fumbled the baton, you do not have to look very far. There are many throughout Scripture.

We want to focus on those who did it right: Jesus, David, Moses, Paul-Timothy, and others.

CHAPTER 5

Timelines are Crucial

One of the most empathic points one of the pastors I interviewed told me was to have very clear timelines. As the pastor assuming the Lead Pastor's role, he shared that his senior pastor was already semi-retiring yet continuing to serve in consulting small churches and pastors—a passion he'd had for many years. This senior pastor now would be moving on to do something he also loved, ministering to small church pastors in his denomination while slowing the pace the senior pastor's role brings.

These two pastors had served together for 25 years. The pastor assuming the church knew his senior pastor well, and the baton handoff was very successful and continues to be. Both pastors are still friends. The senior pastor is still in his church, his parents are in the church, and both still experience a healthy and beautiful relationship, as both told me in separate interviews. The senior pastor who transitioned out still speaks occasionally when in town and is always available when the new pastor needs him or wants to talk. While he did sit in meetings for a while, he moved his office from the church to his home and did not have a leadership role in the church anymore. There were just a few major thoughts each gave that stuck with me very strongly:

The first concerns communication, which we will discuss in the next chapter. The second concerns having very clear timelines. This will help communicate well and reduce misunderstandings, false expectations, and uneasiness about the journey ahead.

Their timeline included a roughly six-year transition but mostly 2-3 years, with the COVID-19 pandemic throwing a wrench into it. They both mentioned holding the timeline loosely since things happen and nothing works out exactly as planned. However, a plan is better than no plan.

I have heard it said for many years:

"Those who fail to plan, plan to fail."

Just this morning, I read this from a young adult, which I thought was very wise and perceptive:

"Be stubborn with the vision. Be flexible with the plan."

Oh, what wisdom!

I look at a timeline more like our annual budget. It gives a map, yet it does not rule or control those who lead and oversee the budget since things change. Seasons sometimes go awry. Giving may drop or expand, and I've witnessed so many other issues in these past 33 years. I could write a book.

Each year, as we go into our annual budget planning with our team, I remind them that just because we give you a budget and approve it does not mean you have the money to spend. Only if the giving and funds come in can we spend them. You all know exactly what I mean. So, on that note, I am sharing with you a proposed timeline here that, in essence, we have already been following for almost two years. We even shared briefly two years ago with the Church Council then as we prepared to bring Pastor Alex (PA) on the team as our Executive Pastor. You will see how we are advancing on the plan, but there is still more ahead.

Proposed Timeline

Years 1-2 (Started October 1, 2022)

Pastor Alex would serve as Executive Pastor. During this time, Pastor Guy will mentor and begin to prepare him for the next steps in our timeline. He would meet on a weekly basis as time allowed. He would be involved in the budgets, leading the staff daily, and hiring new team members. He would do the typical Executive Pastor duties and live out that role while also learning the history, the people, the plans, vision, mission, and other essential DNA pieces of our very special Oasis here in Pembroke Pines.

To my knowledge, there has not been a major decision in any area that was not talked over, prayed over, or considered without PA's input.

Years 3-4 (Begins October 1, 2024)

As we begin year 3 this fall, I believe we should prepare to involve the church in this journey.

I think this part is necessary and gives a *"long runway"* in preparation for the transition and baton handoff. After reading all those books, articles, and interviews, I've concluded that the bigger the church, the longer the *runway* needed. And by runway, I mean time to plan, execute, and prepare for the transition.

This is when there will be more questions than we have answers or that we may want to answer from inquiries of various church attenders and members. Some will say it's too long, and some will say it can be longer. There will be some that might even choose not to go along with this. That is okay, but we must be prepared for it. Knowing Oasis, as I have over 33 years, I am confident the church will accept our leadership decisions, and most will be very excited and show high trust in our next steps.

The real beauty of this is the church already loves and respects PA and his wife, Arelis, so much that they will be very excited. It would not necessarily be true if we said we would bring in someone from outside Oasis with whom no one knows how to take this path. I've seen this stage done several times with outsiders, and sometimes it does not work out. The entire process falls apart during this two-year segment—which, as you already know, I believe is not the best way to transition for all concerned.

Even though I've mentioned this to the Church Council in the past, some of you are new, so the following may or may not be all surprising to you.

Early in this stage, I propose we plan an Ordination Council to interview and interrogate PA with the intent of

Ordination into the Gospel Ministry. Our church has always been very slow to do this and has followed the example of Scripture when Paul informed the church not to "lay hands on any man hastily" (**1 Timothy 5:22**). We have been too slow, perhaps, many times, but I would rather be sure than sorry. Ordination, I believe, is one of the most somber and holy parts of the church since laying hands on a man for lifetime ministry is serious, and like marriage, we own it as a church.

This can be done this January, and the constitution gives me the authority to call for the Ordination Council and to set up the dates and procedures.

In keeping with the Biblical method mentioned previously for choosing our next Lead Pastor for this next season and generation, this next step will launch our formal process of this journey.

The theory of the Co-pastor position is to allow approximately two years shorter, or longer if needed, for our congregation to adjust to a new Lead Pastor. This will enable the new pastor to move into his new position without carrying all the weight of everything all at once, especially since we will also be involved in planning and possibly beginning a new building project—the largest of our 33-year history.

The Co-pastor position is not new among larger churches and works best when the church already knows and loves the pastor who is becoming Co-pastor. In all this, we must not forget the paid staff. One of the most significant fallouts of change in leadership is the paid staff. They are rarely consulted and rarely know the person coming in. They are critical to the success of the church and its future and that of the future pastor. This allows them to adjust to a new leader as well. The advantage of our team is they love and trust PA. He has hired some of them, and he has led all of them for almost two years since the Executive Pastor oversees the staff as delegated by the Senior Pastor.

Co-pastoring would mean that both men make decisions together. With a unity of agreement among important decisions, they would both be on the same page and agree before moving forward. Day-to-day decisions that do not impact monies outside the budget already approved or that will significantly change the direction of the church's future could be made by either one. Both would sign off changes to the constitution, policy for staff, and church-wide plans. Both would carry the weight of the full responsibility of the direction and ministry of Oasis Church.

As with any change or leadership shift, this will not be without challenges. There will be bumps and unexpected challenges.

Here is why I believe we are so well set up for this: I have operated essentially these two years with PA in all these ways. Few—if any—far-reaching churchwide decisions have been made without his complete agreement, or we have not made them.

The Building Beyond initiative was the largest undertaking of our history and at a critical time, not only as a church or during my tenure but also coming off the COVID-19 pandemic. From the beginning, PA was involved in the decisions and directions, and none were made without his signing off on them. No decision of any consequence has been made by me, knowing that we will be coming to this point in two years, the Lord willing. So, we have already functioned this way pretty much for two years. This pathway has allowed us to slowly move me out of the decisions I have been very involved in, like seasonal events, printing, communications, long-term planning, and day-to-day things that PA was already overseeing.

This also frees him to begin planning and navigating Oasis for the future while still having the history and heart of the past by his side.

This timeline allows me to transition my heart and head toward changing roles and stepping out of the Senior and Founding Pastor role. A role I have known for 33 years. It will allow me to concentrate on special projects like

Building Beyond and our missions like Bike for Haiti and Love Cities, Love Pastors. I can better focus on projects to help prepare our church for the future and continue strengthening the foundations of those already established.

For the last two years, much of this has been happening without most knowing it, even though most of the time it has been unsaid. There is hardly anything that PA's fingerprints have not already been on without saying it.

These past two years have allowed us to begin this transition without it being as formal and distracting as it will be, to some extent, naturally. This will not be a significant shift or look to our staff or people since we have unspokenly already been preparing the soil for this next season.

These last two years have been almost too good. They have exceeded my expectations; hopefully, PA will say the same. He has not only met my expectations of what I had hoped for but exceeded them.

I wish I could say there should be an exact passing of the baton, but at this time, I think we should look at two years—give or take—depending on circumstances. That will be how I propose it, allowing for and praying for God's will on the specific timing.

Nothing would make me happier than to build the new building, launch the new ministries, and, on the day we walk into the building, hand the keys to the new pastor and me, being in God's new role for me. I have told PA since the beginning and reiterated it to the architects as they drew the plans not to include an office in the new building for me. I have told them to prepare the Lead Pastor's office however PA wants.

Now, that is the ideal. Sadly, the ideal does not often happen, and my life and ministry experience tell me two years will fly by. If we are fortunate, we will have begun to build the new building in the next two years, not moving into it. Again, these questions and things can prolong this arrangement, but I do not believe they should dictate how we move forward, although they might complicate it.

More on how we might pass the baton and when it'd be in future chapters.

CHAPTER 6

Communication

"Everything rises and falls on communication."

I've heard this statement many times over the years. Sometimes, it's said, "Everything rises and falls on leadership." True, too. This is why I am spending so much energy and time helping us craft a leadership roadmap for the future. We only have one time to do this and do it right.

So maybe we can combine the two statements and say:

"Everything rises and falls on Leadership's Communication."

Good communication is one of the key ingredients to a healthy environment and a successful business or organization.

It is often said that marriages rise and fall depending on how they communicate. In my almost 50 years of ministry and marriage, I would say that communication is vital. The lack of communication can be deadly to any relationship.

I was a little surprised when, in interviews, "communication" came up as the key, if not one of the keys. Every pastor I spoke with and the articles and books I read on transitions and succession planning made this a strong point.

Communication alone is not the answer. It must be well thought out, open, transparent, and appropriate for the message at the right time and place.

I believe our succession and baton transfer will need communication to be a high priority for all of us. The priority in communicating is what I am doing right now. Having a church that has never been down this road with many leaders, maybe even on our Council, who have never had a senior leadership change in our history. *That* is monumental and unique, but it also means we need to work hard at making sure those who need to know certain things hear them straight and not through the grapevine or gossip.

This writing exercise and the months leading up to it have been brutal for me to pray, study, read, and study the Scriptures since it is so personal and might be the single most life-changing decision and step I have made since starting this baby Church in 1991. Maybe more so than that. My emotions have been all over the place. True statement: I had never planned to write a book on this! Until some months ago, I realized this is not something to be done lightly and in one or two Church Council meetings. It will take a lot of planning and communicating like nothing we've ever done before. It feels so personal not only because it's the biggest season of life change in leadership and my calling that I've ever had (or at least, in the last 33 years) but also because Oasis has been all I've known since the little group of 9 men and women joined Tonia and I in a Hallandale mobile home one night in April of 1991, to talk about planting a church. We met at the house of one of our sponsoring pastors, Pastor Jim Washer. Since that day, my life has revolved around Oasis Church and the mission God called me to. The same mission that He has called hundreds of others now, too. I don't want to mess it up. I pray we don't. I pray we handle everything as we go forward in solemn prayer and pleading for God's grace and blessings on this journey.

I'm communicating my heart to you and the road map I think God has revealed to me over the last several years. Then, we will begin communicating with our church family throughout the timeline process that we decide together on.

Prayerfully, we will try to communicate at the right time and place as we move through this process. I believe that with the uniqueness of Oasis Church and the unity God has blessed us with these many years, especially in this season, God will be honored, and the church will continue to reach hundreds and possibly thousands in the next 30 years because of the foundation we lay today.

Communication is key.

CHAPTER 7

The Role of the Church Council

This is a very straight forward chapter but an important one to highlight. However, I find that not much can be said other than the specific Oasis Constitution guidelines already delineated for the vital role of the Church Council in the church.

Article V SECTION 2

THE CHURCH COUNCIL:

(A) The Church council shall consist of a maximum of twelve members who shall assist the Senior Pastor in the planning, financial, and administration functions of the Church. They shall, if requested by the Senior Pastor, consider applications for Church membership. They shall guide day to day ministry activities, **act as the pulpit committee, provide the interim pulpit supply and act as leaders for Church meetings if the office of Senior Pastor is vacant.** The Church council shall assist the Senior Pastor in caring for the administrative needs of the Church's various ministries as requested by the Senior Pastor. They shall annually review and approve the Senior Pastor's salary. They shall approve the Church budget.

Article V SECTION 3

SPECIAL MEETINGS:

(A).... **A meeting for election of a Senior Pastor may be called by the church council for any regular Church meeting of the Church by giving at least two weeks' notice in advance.**

CHURCH COUNCIL:

· Shall consist of a maximum of twelve members who give council and assistance A3, Sec 3, to the Senior Pastor. A5, Sec 2A

· Act with the Senior Pastor as discipline committee A3, Sec 4A

· Approves staff salaries A4, Sec 6A

· Assist the Senior Pastor in the planning, financial and administration A5, Sec 2A

functions of the Church

· If asked by the Senior Pastor, consider applications for membership A5, Sec 2A

· Act as pulpit committee and as leader of church meetings is office of A5, Sec 2A

Senior Pastor is vacant

· Assist the Senior Pastor in caring for the administrative needs of the A5, Sec 2A

Church's various ministries

· Annually review and approve Senior Pastor's salary A5, Sec 2A

· Approve the church budget SecA5, Sec2A

· Constitute the Board of Trustees SecA5, Sec2A

· With the Senior Pastor; designated contributions are subject to the A11

Control and discretion of the Church Council

I have shared these guidelines here to include them as an important part of our Oasis Pastoral Succession Plan. We can move on to the next chapter, where we will discuss *calling* and *changing roles*.

CHAPTER 8

Future Ministry Assignments

I have mentioned not planning to retire. While it sounds good (and some days I'm ready to do it), we have established that retirement day is not biblical for a pastor called by God. Now, I know each of you in your profession plans to retire, and some can do it in their 50s and others in their 60s. I have no issue with that. I'm always happy when a layperson who has worked hard and been faithful gets to retire. That is perfectly fine.

My oldest son is in his mid-40s and can retire in 10 years as a teacher in Seattle with some pretty good benefits. I'm happy for him.

However, without delving into Biblical thoughts about retirement, I know that changing roles is also important.

We all slow down and change, whether we like to admit it or not. Recently, I saw an interview with President Biden, who said he still can't find it within his grasp to say how old he is. (By the way, as I write this, President Biden is 81, almost 82.) None of us ever seem to think we are too old to function effectively unless we have a catastrophic issue, such as a health issue.

So, if the Lord wills it, I'll change roles in the next phase of my ministry. I'm calling it re-tooling, re-imagining, re-treading, re-aligning, or re-positioning, but *not* retiring.

What does this look like? Well, I'm not sure to be exact. There are so many ways to continue ministry as a pastor. I will spare you all of them.

Some are in formal ministry, and some are outside the church or any particular ministry. I prefer to stay in the church ministry since that is my calling, where my strengths and experience lie.

My heart is to pastor. That is my *calling*.

I've pastored in many ways: children's pastor, youth pastor, education pastor, associate pastor, church planter, founding pastor, and senior pastor.

Thinking within a local church environment like Oasis, I can see my role changing to concentrate on smaller and more focused ministry. What could that look like, using Oasis as an example? During these two years, Pastor Alex and our Oasis Council will determine that.

CHAPTER 9

Senior Pastor's Commitment to the Church, Leadership, and Lead Pastor

I feel that, along with the succession timelines and other important considerations, regardless of how we decide to go with so many options open to us, I should give some assurance of how I plan to act after my *re-positioning* and stepping away from Lead, or Senior Pastor as we know it.

One of the greatest land mines and issues when pastors leave, whether by death, retirement, or re-assignments, is how they interact with the future church leadership and congregation. As mentioned previously, one of the reasons most pastors leave a church altogether, even if they are living locally and not pastoring, is because of the unhealthy cultural way we vote on, pick, and hire new pastors. I know no one ever goes into a transition—whether the pastor, the church, or the new pastor—with the idea there are going to be issues or problems. There is also an idealistic view: we are a church, and all love each other. Ha! We are all still on this side of heaven (and still carry our sinful nature living in our present bodies) just as Paul, Barnabas, and other early Christians were in the early church. Yet the Bible says that there came "Disputes, divisions, whining, and gossip." You name it. I pray, hope, and wish by all the planning we will do and by prayerfully executing a succession and transition plan, that we can avoid this, as many churches have.

Doing it the most Biblical way that I have laid out previously still means personalities, conflict, and other negatives can happen. Because of that, based on my experience, learning, and watching so many churches, I feel that I should put in writing some commitments to you, our church, and our new Lead Pastor.

My commitment to God, Oasis Church, and our new Lead Pastor:

1. I will always work to uphold the values, vision, and mission of Oasis Church in word and deed.
2. I will respect the past, the present, and the future with my words and actions.
3. I will always hold up our beloved church in my thoughts and prayers.
4. I will never speak ill of the Council, the Lead Pastor, or any leadership, even if I disagree with them.
5. If I have an issue I feel strongly about, I will only approach the person.
6. I will never listen to or participate in gossip with others about the present leadership or pastor.
7. I will always support the pastor's vision and philosophy, and if there were ever a theological issue we could not resolve, I would quietly leave if necessary. I do not believe a pastor or member who has stepped down or left should ever be part of rumors, gossip, and negative vibes in a church. This is unbiblical, and God will judge those who do.
8. I will willingly relinquish all control and leadership of my present position, not trying to hold on to it or to distract from the new Lead Pastor.
9. I will not discuss, talk about, or entertain any staff members' complaints, grievances, or issues with the church leadership and Lead Pastor. The

Scriptural thing to do is to send them directly to where there is an issue.

10. I will always be our new pastor's biggest cheerleader, privately and publicly.
11. I will support the work of Oasis, Building Beyond, Bike for Haiti, and Love Cities, Love Pastors as long as I am a part of the church, serving and giving.
12. I will be available as much as humanly possible if the new pastor asks me to assist or give advice, history, or context.
13. I will not give unsolicited advice to the new leadership.
14. I will live by the same Membership Covenant our Oasis Church family agrees to when they become members.

These are not exclusive and all that I want to assure the church leadership, but they are what I can think of now. I'm sure there may be more, or if you ask me about other areas, I'm happy to make reasonable assurances, knowing none of us is perfect. I can't say I won't fail or stumble sometimes, but I know what it means to be the Senior and Lead guy, and only someone who has been there can understand the pressure, stress, and pain it is to lead a large church, large staff, and a diverse community.

CHAPTER 10

Next Steps

While I have already shared some thoughts on the succession timeline, in this chapter I want to add a little more meat to it. Again, let me remind us that our timing is not always God's, and plans and timelines can change based on circumstances. As Tonia says, "Man plans, and God laughs." However, if we fail to plan, we plan to fail, right?

We are still at the beginning point, not the ending or final steps in our plan, for sure. However, I'll try to answer what you might want to ask as you read through this Pastoral Succession Plan.

Let me reiterate, it's only a *rough draft*.

Here is a more detailed description of our next steps in our timeline:

FALL 2024

<u>September</u>—**The rough draft of the Pastoral Succession Plan has been completed** and handed to our Council and a few select leaders who have previously served on the Council. Council members are asked to read this before our October meeting.

<u>October</u>—**We will discuss the plan, make any changes** that we might want or need to make, **and vote on the general plan. The Council will work on details** moving forward.

<u>November</u>—Continue to discuss and work on final details to be decided before Christmas at the Oasis when things get crazy since I would like our timeline for transition to officially begin in January of 2025 after the Christmas season.

<u>December</u>—**The focus is on Christmas at the Oasis, and the Senior Pastor and Executive Pastor begin to plan our next steps**, which should begin in January.

January—*Ordination Council* ordains Pastor Alex. (This Ordination Council comprises ordained pastors within and without the church who share the same theological and ecclesiastical beliefs. The Senior Pastor is tasked with putting it together.) There are precise steps we take in formally ordaining a man into ministry. We will follow those we have used in years past when we have ordained men like Kevin McCord, Jeremy Higdon, and Duane Oyer. This is a very important and sober step. Pastor Alex is already licensed, a precursor to Ordination, and more of a state and financial step for future and present pastors. Also, licensing during the Fall will be done on Colin Sprouse's behalf to move him from Youth Director to Youth Pastor, an essential step toward his life calling as a youth pastor. He will not be ordained immediately until the pastoral team is ready to call for that.

February—The beginning of the two years of sharing the pastorate as co-pastors has already been laid out. During these two years, I will begin to transition out of the day-to-day and be seen less publicly as the leader but more as the *baton passer*.

2025-2026—This is where things get less clear, murkier, and harder to predict a timetable. While I've mentioned I would prefer to finish building our new building before we make the final handoff, our country's financial and cultural issues may not allow us to move that fast.

I do not want to overstay my welcome and hold back the future, but I don't want to abandon our future leaders and church to have the biggest project in our history before us.

This is where we will have to pray and evaluate as we go. More than likely, most of the leaders making these most weighty decisions in our church's history won't be on the Council to make those final decisions. This is the hard part.

But it is with the Church Council that we will keep talking and evaluating conditions and PA. I will constantly monitor how he feels and what timeline he prefers. Then, together, we will make a decision and bring it to the Council for discussion. Now, again, all this could change. Two to three years is an eternity these days when the whole world changes sometimes in 24 hours, and the economy is very fragile and could either boom the next couple of years or crash. Only God knows.

If the ideal succession plan were to happen, we would finish the building sometime in 2026. I would take my final sabbatical to give the transition a chance for the new pastor to get settled in, and then the next Chapter of the Oasis Story and mine would begin. That is the ideal. However, I don't see how that happens at this point, but you must at least think through it and have a plan.

CONCLUSION: Roots

"One generation will declare Your works to the next and will proclaim Your mighty acts." (Psalm 145:4)

So many things can be said about *roots*. Sermons and books about roots exist, and while they are not seen on the surface, they are probably the most important part of the life-giving strength of any tree.

Family roots are beautiful, but for many, they are damaged, shallow, or non-existent. That is a tragedy. It is also a tragedy when a church that has existed for many years (many times, even a century) has damaged root systems or separated roots that weaken the branches and the trunk.

So many churches have had splits, multiple pastors, deep hurts, and losses. I would say that is more common in the North American Church than we hear about. Thankfully, you may be surprised at these words since you have been blessed to be in a church with strong roots that go deep into the soil and stretch way beyond Pembroke Pines.

Most churches, somewhere along the way, lose the baby and tender roots they had when birthed and don't get to pass the Mission and Vision from one generation to another, decade after decade. I grieve for them.

I feel so blessed that while my family roots of an alcoholic dad were damaged early on, the roots of my church I grew up in are not just still there but eternally intertwined with Oasis.

Flying from Brazil many years ago from a mission trip late at night, 35,000 feet above sea level, a young man who had grown up in my youth group and on the mission field of Brazil said something I've never forgotten, and yet I don't think I've ever shared before.

Ken McCord—who happens to be the oldest son of our missionary and sending and sponsoring pastor 33 years ago—mentioned roots to me during that flight I will always remember. He shared how thankful he was to have strong roots in the faith. Ken and his wife Kellie, one of my all-time favorite young people during my ten years as a youth pastor in my home church (now called Hollywood Community in West Hollywood, Florida,) moved to San Francisco 20 years ago. They left the comfort of Brazil and Florida to embark on the inner city of San Francisco and bring the seeds of the Gospel to the people in one of our country's most spiritually dead cities. They are still there today.

Having only been there a few years, Ken shared how important having roots was to him. His roots come from a Godly family and Godly people in the church where he grew up in West Hollywood. He mentioned how those roots have given him and Kelly the strength to carry on in a distant city with no family or friends within thousands of miles. He noted that while his family wasn't perfect and our church in West Hollywood was far from ideal, the passing of the baton from one generation to the next and the next brought continuity to the ministry.

He went on to say that even though he hardly ever sees me or many of the leaders he grew up with, a strong past and connected roots, are among his biggest blessings.

What a beautiful testimony.

This is what I want Oasis to continue. See, we are an extension of that ministry that birthed us. And the root thread continues with other churches like City Rev in Western Pines, which we helped birth. City Rev has now sent one of their young men to succeed the present pastor at my home church to continue the root system. What an incredible family of God we are part of!

This is one of the reasons it's so vital for me to pass the baton off to another Oasiser. One who loves our church, our people, the story of Oasis, our Mission, and our Vision. Yet one that represents new growth, new generations, and fresh potential for the years, decades, and generations to come. While I begin to wrap up what was only going to be a few pages early in the process, this missal is more than emotional for me, and, at times, I've had a wrenching feeling in my gut to know that the reality of a life of almost 50 years of ministry—the way I have known it—is coming to a close. I have another 50 years of dreams and vision, yet this will be for the next generation of Oasis leaders to draw and sketch out in their own way and time. I'm at peace with that.

Many pastors leave early because of burnout or other catastrophic events, some of them financial. Then, others stay too long because of the pats on the back, leadership incentives, and finances. You leave early, you hurt the church and fall short of your calling; you leave too late, and you hurt the church and your own calling. Both are harmful. So, when do you leave? When God makes it abundantly clear, and you have peace about it. (No pressures to leave, no ulterior motives, no push or crisis.

Although all those things can somehow play a part.) God had to make me extremely uncomfortable before leaving my beloved home church where I grew up and served for 13 years to start Oasis Church in 1991.

I've explained it like the making of a pearl. The pearl isn't made without the sand and irritation inside the shell over some time. I've called my calling to start Oasis, a 2x4 hit over the head by God since I resisted for over a year.

Many transitions are messy and contentious. Divisions between factions and the void between leaders with no planning or succession plan from the Senior or Lead pastor to the next one, create a void where Satan can attack, and so many churches lose momentum, people they need not lose, or pain they need not endure.

I do not intend to let that happen if I can help it in my beloved *Oasis* where I have spent the better part of my ministry. This is the reason for this long book—which happens to be the shortest book I've ever written, ha. At least it does not have 500 pages like *Brown Bag Prayers*. ;)

I love you, Oasis.

Now, let us go **Build Beyond**.

APPENDIX

As I was getting ready to send my manuscript to be published, I happened to be looking for a book in my office library when, by "accident," I pulled out a different book I had read many years ago: *Leadership Prayers* by Richard Kriegbaum[8]. I don't think it was a coincidence; I had circled "Succession Prayer" in the index and took a few notes. I would love to share a few highlighted excerpts that had become my prayer long before I planned this book.

****

> SUCCESSION: I will not last forever, God. Where are my replacements?
>
> Jesus called his twelve disciples to him and gave them authority. Matthew 10:1
>
> As soon as the vision is announced, the leader must begin succession planning and selection, just as Jesus did.
>
> In June after my twelfth year at Fresno Pacific University, my wife, Elona, and I drove to the coast for our annual day of considering

---

[8] Richard Kriegbaum, *Leadership Prayers* (Tyndale, n.d.).

whether the fiscal year just starting should be my last in the role of president. That day, as always, I spent time on each element of the succession prayer. I asked myself whether what yet needed to be done still sent eager fire through my belly. I envisioned other leaders in my place. I relived my successes and faced the things I had gotten wrong or left undone. The institution was maturing beautifully, and I felt that my evolving leadership could meet the emerging needs. I pondered where we were, Elona and I, on the path of our own pilgrimage as individuals and as a couple.

By midday I had to admit that I had no peace about continuing. The years ahead looked wonderful, but I could no longer see myself as the president. We were both stunned to silence. In the weeks that followed, we began to see that God had completed what he had called us there to do, and in October I resigned. It was the single most difficult—and most important—decision of my tenure. Subsequent years confirmed that I had gotten it right. It was good for the university and good for me. Leadership succession plays out in the departure of the incumbent, and departing well depends on intentional prayer.

(The Succession Prayer)

I can help prepare leaders, and I can help the organization be ready for them.

Show me the ones who challenge me, the ones with more freedom and stronger faith than I have. Point out the ones who love people better than I do, who lead because they really care about people. Make the spiritual giants visible to me. Let me notice the ones who attract loyal, high-quality friends.

Help me distinguish between the confident and the arrogant, between the humble and the hesitant. Bring out the strong ones who can carry their own burdens and also the burdens of others. Allow tough times that will yield success to those who refuse to give up. Help me advance the leaders for the future.

Oh, God of mercy, don't let me stay in this job one day too long . . .

I will not last forever, God. Where are my replacements?

Help me remember, God, that I can be reassigned, neutralized, or eliminated for a thousand different reasons at any moment. My leadership is precarious, hanging by the silver thread of people's trust in me. Countless things over which I have no control can break that thread, including your call elsewhere, and I will be gone.

But they need a leader, and when I am gone they must have others to turn to, others whom they trust, who can tell them the truth. Show me those who can lead after me and better than me. Ruffle my spirit when they are near, quicken my heart when I feel their power, and open my eyes to see the special effect they have on people.

Protect me from preserving my own position or power or perspectives at the expense of future leaders. When they point out where I have not led well, shut my mouth and open my heart. Help me make it safe for them to try new things. Let me touch the spirit of those who possess the heart of a servant. I want to know them and love them and watch their energy flow into others around them. I want to claim them for this work and pray them into my place . . .

Amen.

Statistics of Pastors in the United States

- **38%** of pastors are thinking of quitting the ministry, **51%** from mainline denominations. (November 29, 2021) Of the **38%**, almost half **(46%)** are under age **45**. **50%** of pastors are age 56 and above. 2022 stats reveal a rise from **38% to 42%**.
- **85%** of pastors believe the mission of the church is to reach the lost, only 42% of practicing Christians do.
- **72%** of the pastors report working between **55** to **75** hours per week. **(Pre-Covid-19)**
- **84%** of pastors feel they are on call 24/7.
- 80% believe pastoral ministry has negatively affected their families. Many pastor's children do not attend church now because of what the church has done to their parents.
- **65%** of pastors feel their family lives in a "glass house" and fear they are not good enough to meet expectations.
- **23%** of pastors report being distant from their family.
- **78%** of pastors report having their vacation and personal time interrupted by ministry duties or expectations.
- **65%** of pastors feel they have <u>not</u> taken enough vacation time with their family over the last 5 years.
- 28% of pastors report having feelings of guilt for taking personal time off and not telling the church.

- **35%** of pastors report the demands of the church deny them from spending time with their families.
- **24%** of pastor's families resent the church and its effect on their family.
- **22%** of pastor's spouses report the ministry places undue expectations on their family.
- **66%** of church members **expect** a minister and family to live at a higher moral standard than themselves.
- **53%** of pastors report that the seminary did not prepare them for the ministry.
- **90%** of pastors report the **ministry was completely different** than what they thought it would be like before they entered the ministry.
- **45%** of pastors spend 10-15 hours a week on sermon preparation.
- **85%** of pastors report the use of the internet and other resources have improved their study time compared to when they first started their ministry.
- **50%** of pastors state they spend 1 hour in prayer each day.
- **57%** of pastors believe they do not receive a livable wage.
- **57%** of pastors being unable to pay their bills.
- **53%** of pastors are concerned about their future family financial security.
- **75%** of pastors report significant **stress-related** crisis at least once in their ministry.

- **80%** of pastors and **84%** of their spouses have felt unqualified and discouraged as role of pastors at least one or more times in their ministry.
- **52%** of pastors feel overworked and cannot meet their church's unrealistic expectations.
- **54%** of pastors find the role of a pastor overwhelming.
- **40%** report serious conflict with a parishioner at least **once in the last year.**
- **80%** of pastors expect conflict within their church.
- **75%** of pastors report spending 4-5 hours a week in needless meetings.
- **35%** of pastors battle depression or fear of inadequacy.
- **26%** of pastors report being overfatigued.
- **28%** of pastors report they are spiritually undernourished.
- Over **50%** of pastors state the biggest challenge is to recruit volunteers and encourage their members to change (living closer to God's Word).
- **70%** of pastors report they have a **lower self-image now** than when they first started.
- **70%** of pastors do not have someone they consider to be a close friend.
- **27%** of pastors report not having anyone to turn to for help in a crisis situation.
- **57%** of pastors feel fulfilled but yet discouraged, stressed, and fatigued.

- **84%** of pastors desire to have close fellowship with someone they can trust and confide with.
- Over **50%** of pastors are unhealthy, overweight, and do <u>not</u> exercise.
- The **profession of "Pastor"** is near the bottom of a survey of the most-respected professions, just above **"car salesman."**
- **Many denominations are reporting an "Empty Pulpit Crisis." They do not have a shortage of ministers but have a shortage of ministers desiring to fill the role of a pastor.**
- **71%** of churches have no plan for a pastor to receive a periodic sabbatical.
- **66%** of churches have no lay counseling support.
- **30%** of churches have no documentation clearly outlining what the church expects of their pastor.
- **1 out of every 10 pastors will actually retire as a pastor.**

Improvements:

- **73%** of churches are treating their pastors better. This statistic has improved due to the advent of clergy appreciation, better education on the role of the pastor, and denominational awareness to better supporting their pastors.

- **77%** of pastors, especially millennials (younger pastors ages usually born around 1978-1990), are spending 20 or more hours with their families each week.
- **90%** of pastors feel they are called and in the place where God has called them.

New Statistics:

- Gallop poll (April 2022) reveals that **46%** of Americans believe church is important to them now, down from **70%** for decades. More people now believe church is not important to them.
- Gallup poll states there has been a **10-point drop** in attendance from the previous decade. **45%** of American adults say they attend religious services, an all-time low.
- **50%** of Americans state they are members of a church. **36%** say they have confidence in church or organized religion.

New Pastoral Statistics:

- Barna reports **85%** of pastors believe the mission of the church is to reach the lost, only **42%** of practicing Christians feel the same.
- **Barna reports that 42% of pastors are thinking of leaving the ministry in 2022.**
- **Barna reports 38% of pastors are thinking of quitting the ministry, 51% from mainline denominations. November 29, 2021.**
- **Covid-19 brought many things to a breaking point. Ministry can take its toll. It's never been this bad. Edify leaders, October 2021.**

Older Statistics Still Being Researched for Current Numbers:

- **4,000 new churches begin each year, and 7,000 churches close.**
- **Over 1,500 pastors left the ministry every month last year.**
- **Over 1,300 pastors were terminated by the local church each month, many without cause.**
- Over **3,500** people **a day** left the church last year.

Assembled by Pastoral Care Inc.

BIBLIOGRAPHY

- *The Magnificent Exit*, By Neil Hart
- *Succession: Preparing your Ministry for the Next Leader* by Bryant Wright
- *Where Will the Mantle Fall? A Biblical and Legal Guide to Succession Planning*, by Travell Travis
- *Tsunami: Open Secrets to Pastoral Succession & Transition,* by Samuel R Chand and Scott Wilson

Made in the USA
Columbia, SC
07 February 2025

52796548R10062